inner curtain wall
with galleries

watchtower

stables

garden

dovecote

domestic courtyard   baking oven

curtain wall

outpost

mantlet wall

D1511542

3

First published in England in 1989 by
Young Library Ltd
45 Norfolk Square, Brighton
East Sussex BN1 2PE

Text © Copyright 1989 Young Library Ltd
Illustrations © Copyright 1986
Altberliner Verlag, Berlin
All rights reserved

ISBN 0 946003 92 0

Printed in the German Democratic Republic

Introducing Castles

Text by Christiane Bimberg
Illustrations by Thomas Binder

In ancient times people began to fortify their homes against attackers. They made palisades of timber around their villages, or cleverly built their houses on platforms in the middle of lakes. As time went by they learned better ways of building, and used stone instead of wood. The walls grew higher and thicker. The strongest buildings of all were the castles.

During the Middle Ages, thousands of castles stood proudly all over Europe. You have probably seen the centuries-old remains of some of these castles. Perhaps you have wondered what forgotten secrets they held. For behind those massive stone walls, now so grim and silent, people lived out their everyday lives just as if they were living in any small town.

Young Library

In the days of the ancient Greeks, Romans, and Celtic peoples of northern Europe, various kinds of fortified buildings were already offering shelter in times of emergency. We can still see the ruins of many Roman fortresses. About 1,000 years ago the first medieval castles were built, and they soon spread over most of Europe. It is astonishing to imagine what gigantic amounts of stone had to be heaved around, with the simplest machinery, and what an enormous effort it must have taken to build these castles. High, thick walls, pierced by only narrow slits to let in light and to allow bowmen to shoot arrows out, were built to give protection against the enemy's siege machines. There was a gradual change in the appearance of castles, as architectural fashions and military tactics both developed.

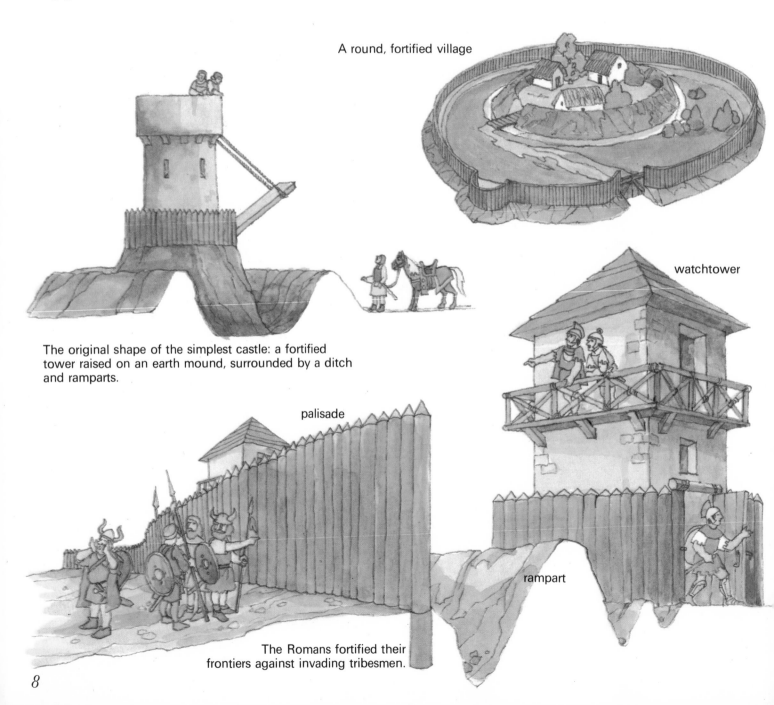

A round, fortified village

The original shape of the simplest castle: a fortified tower raised on an earth mound, surrounded by a ditch and ramparts.

watchtower

palisade

rampart

The Romans fortified their frontiers against invading tribesmen.

Each country began to develop its own style of building. In Spain citadels were built with double walls with rooms inside. In Italy different members of a noble family would live each in their own towers. In England the Normans built castles with a square central tower standing by itself in the middle of a walled enclosure; this was called the 'keep'. Building styles tried out in one country were often copied elsewhere. For example, in the twelfth and thirteenth centuries, European Crusaders returned from wars in the Middle East. They brought back with them the idea of an extra outer wall to increase the defences by making a 'ward' or circular space between two ring walls. Castles began to take on an individual appearance, as gradual improvements were made and extensions were built.

Norman castle at
Newcastle-upon-Tyne, England, in about 1080.

Castel del Monte, Italy, in about 1240; this shows Arab styles learned during the Crusades.

The massive castle of Tarascon, France, built between the 12th and 15th centuries.

The harbour tower of Belem, Portugal, in about 1520.

Ideally a castle should only have one side open to attack. The road up to the castle was made narrow, so that only a few soldiers could approach together. The road was curved so that attackers had their right side – the side not covered by a shield – facing towards the castle, so that they were vulnerable to arrows. Platforms, protected by battlements to give cover to the defenders, ran along the tops of the walls. These were sometimes roofed over with timber galleries. Archers could shoot in safety through narrow slits. Overlooking the approaches were galleries with 'murder-holes' in the floor, through which the defenders could pour down boiling water, tar, and sulphur to scald and burn attackers. It was not until later medieval times that much thought was given to domestic comfort when building a castle.

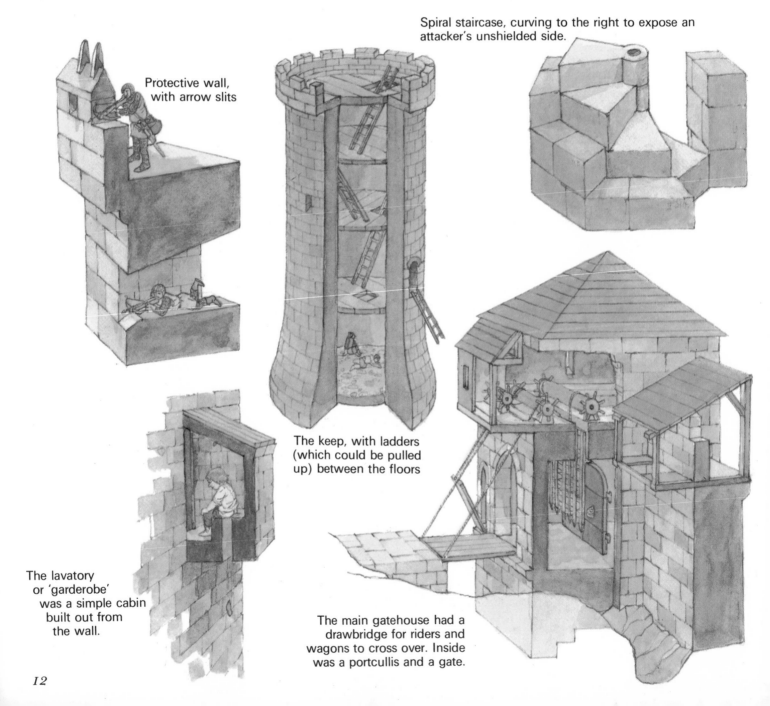

Protective wall, with arrow slits

Spiral staircase, curving to the right to expose an attacker's unshielded side.

The keep, with ladders (which could be pulled up) between the floors

The lavatory or 'garderobe' was a simple cabin built out from the wall.

The main gatehouse had a drawbridge for riders and wagons to cross over. Inside was a portcullis and a gate.

The last refuge for defenders in time of siege was inside the multi-storey keep. It was usually built of stone, with an entrance high above the ground.

The lowest floor of the keep served as a prison; higher up were store rooms; and higher still were the living quarters. Once the location for a castle had been chosen, the builder hired the number of craftsmen he needed. Wood, stone, sand, ironware, and tools were transported to the site. Several thousand workers would be employed in the building. There were ditch-diggers, stonemasons, cement- and mortar-mixers, bricklayers, carpenters, blacksmiths, plumbers, and labourers to fetch and carry. Even in those days builders used machinery to supplement human muscle-power. There were simple wooden scaffolding with bridges, rollers, pulleys, and winches.

carpenters

wood drill

stone-chisel

carpenter's axe

stone masons' hammer

wedge

stone-cutters

simple crane

stonemason

15

A series of ramparts, ditches, and other obstacles were built to make it very difficult for an enemy to break into the castle. Gates were protected by towers, and some became so elaborate that the gatehouse formed a sort of small castle of its own, separate from the main buildings.

A drawbridge – which could be raised or lowered on chains by the defenders from inside – crossed the moat at the main entrance. There were sometimes smaller drawbridges inside, allowing the defenders to isolate the different parts of the castle if one area were captured. If the castle was subjected to a siege, the attackers used various powerful machines in their attempts to break through the walls. Catapults, called 'ballistas' or 'mangonels', could hurl large arrows, stones, fire-pots, or even more imaginative things like

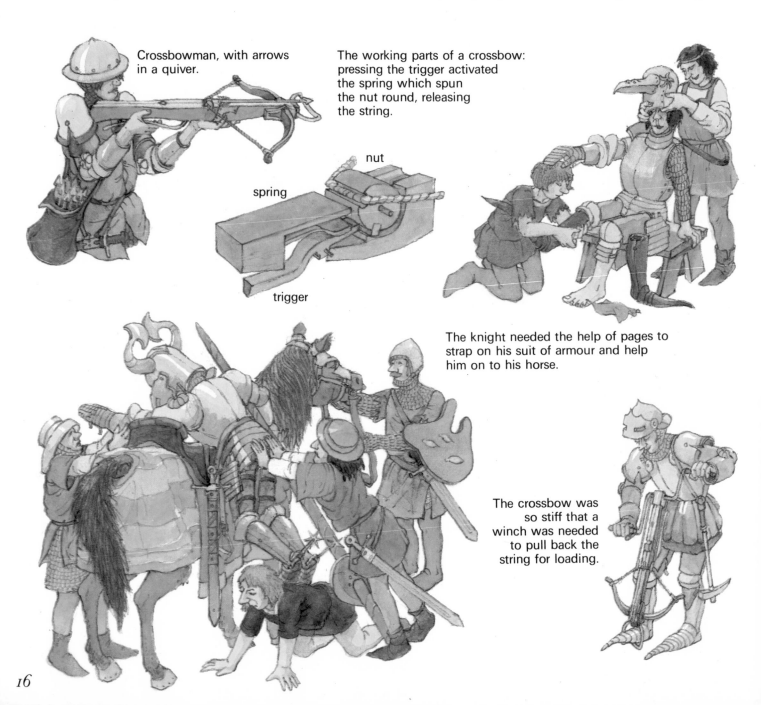

Crossbowman, with arrows in a quiver.

The working parts of a crossbow: pressing the trigger activated the spring which spun the nut round, releasing the string.

nut

spring

trigger

The knight needed the help of pages to strap on his suit of armour and help him on to his horse.

The crossbow was so stiff that a winch was needed to pull back the string for loading.

hives of angry bees over the walls into the castle. Under cover of temporary wooden roofs, miners would try to tunnel under the outer walls.

Various types of battering ram – often with names like 'cat', 'mouse', or 'sow', from the shapes of the iron heads fitted to the swinging beams – were swung back and forth to break down gates and walls. Mobile wooden towers were pushed up against walls and towers, and from their tops archers shot arrows to clear the defenders from the ramparts. They also shot fire-arrows to set the defences ablaze, for many of the galleries and interior buildings were made of wood. If the attackers managed to clamber from the towers, or up scaling-ladders, and get inside the walls, hand-to-hand fighting broke out. If one of the main gates was captured, the defenders were in real difficulty.

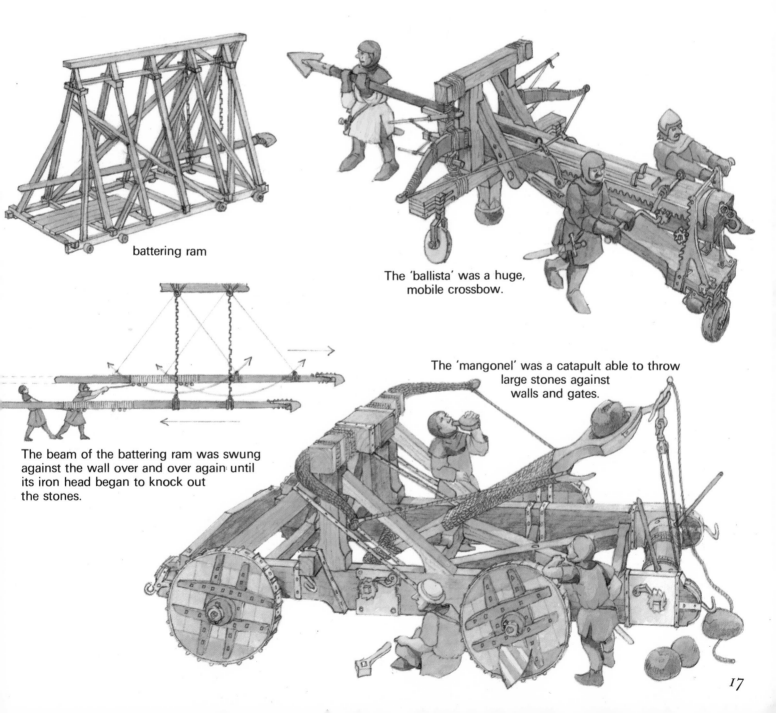

battering ram

The 'ballista' was a huge, mobile crossbow.

The beam of the battering ram was swung against the wall over and over again until its iron head began to knock out the stones.

The 'mangonel' was a catapult able to throw large stones against walls and gates.

The castle contained all the necessities of life: it had stables and barns, workshops and smithies, and storehouses for provisions of all kinds. Many servants were employed to look after the needs of the nobleman's family. There was a chief cook, with several helpers. The steward supervised the preparation of food, and the serving at table. There was a cellarer in charge of the wine, and the cup-bearers who served it. The marshal was responsible for the stables and horses. The treasurer took care of the castle's valuables. Washerwomen and maidservants did the laundry, and the spinning and sewing for new clothes. Scholars were employed by those nobles who thought it necessary for their children to learn to read and write. All these people lived inside the castle, or in houses just outside the walls.

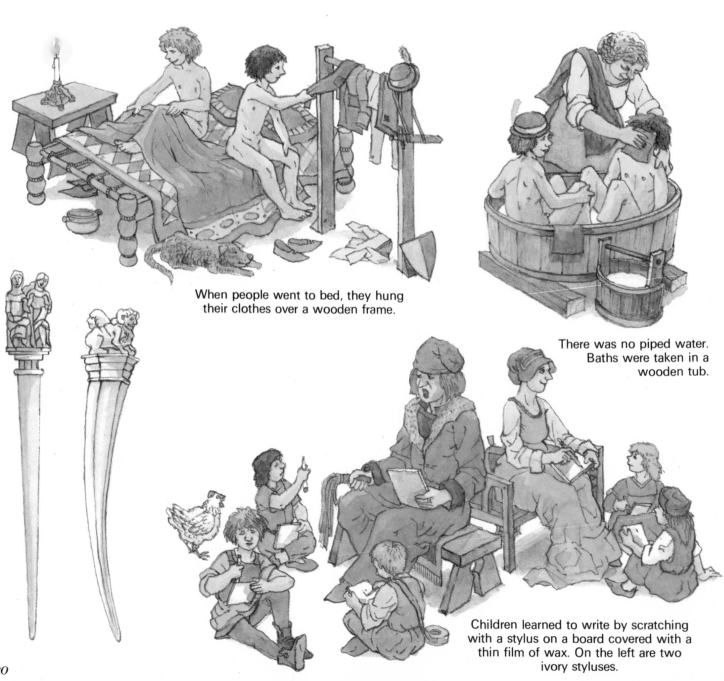

When people went to bed, they hung their clothes over a wooden frame.

There was no piped water. Baths were taken in a wooden tub.

Children learned to write by scratching with a stylus on a board covered with a thin film of wax. On the left are two ivory styluses.

The nobleman's children were taught grown-up skills from quite an early age. The girls learned how to supervise the running of a household, while the boys were taught how to handle weapons and horses. Often the boys would be sent away to live at a neighbouring castle, to complete their education and improve their manners. A very popular pastime for nobles was hunting. They chased deer from horseback accompanied by dogs, or used trained falcons to attack other birds in mid-air. When travelling, most people walked, but nobles rode on horseback or in litters. Roads were muddy, rutted, and sometimes unsafe because of lurking outlaws, so journeys were often exhausting and quite dangerous. Usually noble ladies stayed behind. Fine embroidery was their main pastime.

Riding out to hunt with falcons; the court jester has come along too.

Boys playing with jousting puppets.

Noble ladies work at their embroidery.

21

In spite of all the efforts to make castle life comfortable, it must have been fairly hard. In cold weather, draughts must have whistled in around the shutters and parchment screens which covered the unglazed windows. No wonder everyone looked forward to spring and summer, when they could enjoy themselves outside. Every chance to hold a celebration – weddings, christenings, the knighting of young squires, even funerals – was seized eagerly. Guests would come from near and far, bringing longed-for news and gossip. Preparations for the feast were started many weeks in advance. Livestock had to be bought in; the dressmaker had to be given orders for festive clothing; gifts had to be bought for all the guests, and all the best furniture, hangings and cutlery had to be got out and cleaned. Messengers

Dancers follow the lead of a fiddler.

Travelling minstrels, jugglers, and conjurers provided entertainment.

Chess was also played in the garden.

rode off to deliver the invitations. Everybody took the opportunity to show off their finest new clothes.

A rich court attracted the best artists: poets and minstrels found a welcome and generous audience for their verses, music and songs. Great attention was paid to good manners and chivalry, and exaggerated respect was paid to ladies, as perfect examples of womankind.

The climax of many festivities was the tournament, a mock fight between knights on horseback or on foot which took place in a fenced arena, or in the castle courtyard. There were the most rigid rules for the conduct of these display-bouts; but in the heat of fighting the contest sometimes turned into a more bitter and bloody event than was intended. Knights were quite often killed in these tournaments.

The 'solar', the family's private quarters, served as bedroom, nursery, and living room. Clothes were stored in wooden chests.

In the chapel the lord's family stood in the gallery, lesser folk assembled below.

The power of the lords lasted for about 500 years. Towards the end of this period the castles became less important. New weapons and tactics began to govern warfare. The invention of gunpowder and cannon meant that no castle, however strong, could withstand attack for very long. Wars were more often fought by large armies moving about the open countryside. In private feuds, national wars, and various uprisings by peasants and townspeople, many castles were destroyed.

At the same time, life in towns and villages steadily improved. The growth in trade of all kinds brought greater wealth to the towns. A merchant class grew up which challenged the tyranny of the lords in their castles. As towns grew larger and richer, they too were fortified with strong walls. Castles changed. Instead of

A peasant family paying their taxes in foodstuffs.

The simple peasant shoe became the symbol of a peasant uprising in Germany in 1492–1514.

Rebellious peasants, with their 'shoe' standard.

Some of the fearsome weapons used by footsoldiers: spiked war flails and 'morning stars'.

being homes for a wealthy family and its servants, they were gradually replaced by fortresses built purely as military garrisons, designed in quite a different way, and mounting cannon themselves.

A few of the old castles were slowly altered and rebuilt purely as homes for the aristocracy, with no defensive value. However, many were allowed to decay into ruins. It was not until about 200 years ago that the splendour of castles began to be appreciated. Today many of them house museums, art galleries, even hotels or restaurants.

The sight of even ruined castles remains impressive. The castles' roofs may long ago have fallen in, and the wind may whistle round their broken walls; their ditches may have become filled with rubble; but they still stand, witnesses to a stormy past.

Thieves and swindlers were locked into the stocks in the marketplace, for all to see.

A merchant at his counting table.

Traders and craftsmen offered all kinds of wares for sale in the town markets.